Benorth Forth

The Aichils cheynge aa dey.
Cheyngin lichts ay pley
Apon Aichils' backs,
An cluds mak tracks.

Mair cheynge nor thon they shaw's:
Gerss, hedder, moss,
Tree, buss an flou'er
Cheynge by the hour.

Snaw, hailstanes, rain wull beat;
Thir, an the sun's heat.
Haar silken haps them roun;
Cluds, hooker - doun...

This orra reynge,
Under the chairge o cheynge
Is life-in-brief —
An like life, pruif!

David Angus

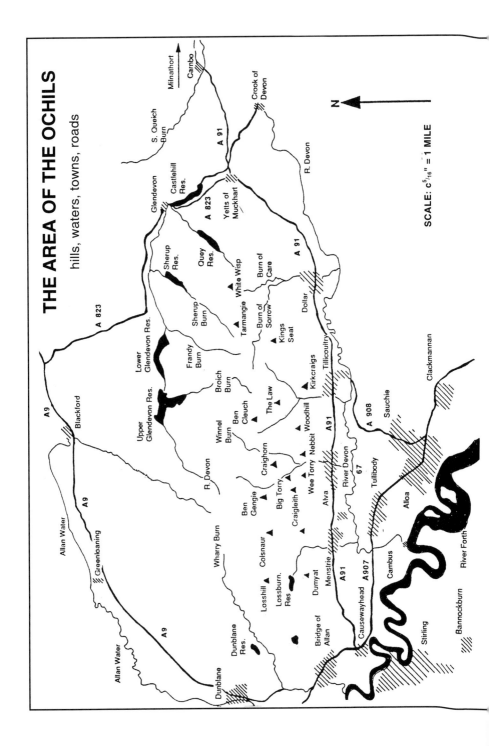

THE AREA OF THE OCHILS
hills, waters, towns, roads

N

SCALE: c⁵/₁₆" = 1 MILE

THE OCHIL HILLS

An Introduction

Landscape, Wildlife, Heritage, Walks

L. Corbett

E. K. Roy

R.C. Snaddon

Forth Naturalist and Historian

and

Clackmannanshire Field Studies Society

First published by The Forth Naturalist and Historian and the Clackmannanshire Field Studies Society, 1994.
The Forth Naturalist and Historian is a Stirling University/Central Regional Council collaboration (Honorary Editor/Secretary L. Corbett).

Clackmannan District Arts Council, Central Regional Council and Stirling District Council have made contributions towards printing costs.

British Library Cataloguing in Publication Data

Corbett, L. et al
Ochil Hills: Introduction - Landscape, Wildlife, Heritage, Walks.
I. Title
914.12 804

ISBN 0 9506962 3 4 (FN&H)
ISBN 0 9036500 7 X (CFSS)

Design Consultant - G. Thomson

Text, in 10pt Times; and production copy by Central Region Education Advisers and L. Corbett.
Cover Artist Jennifer Campbell. Line Drawings by E.K. Roy
.
Printed by Cordfall, Glasgow 041 332 4640

CONTENTS

INTRODUCTION

The Ochils is an outstanding feature of the Central Scotland landscape. A number of publications already deal with particular aspects e.g. walks, mill trail, mines and minerals, woollen mill buildings; legends and history of Menzies Fergusson and Rennie McOwan, and walks with Richard Bernard. A first draft some years ago by Bob Snaddon made us realise the need for an introductory booklet to give some basic information on the range of naturalist and historical characteristics of these hills.

It is hoped that this short survey might be a welcome environmental introduction, add a little knowledge to the pleasure of viewing the landscape, and perhaps stimulate deeper interests. We would welcome comments useful towards its further development.

ACKNOWLEDGEMENTS

We are grateful for the contributions and comments of numerous people mostly named in the text, verso of title page and at poems, drawings, photos; also to Ian Lindsay of Ochils Mountain Rescue, Tourist Board for its 'approval' logo, Clackmannanshire Field Studies Society for forbearance with the lengthy 'gestation' time of production, and J. Gallacher (SNH) and R. McOwan for helpful comments.

1 SAFETY AND BEHAVIOUR IN THE HILLS

The Ochils, particularly the southern parts, have many precipitous slopes, and rocks are often weathered into loose and dangerous areas. These and unstable scree are best avoided. In many places it is not advisable to stray from the footpaths, particularly in wooded glens. Steep grass slopes above bluffs can be dangerous particularly after rain.

Sensible warm clothing and stout footwear should be worn.

Always have some food, a torch, and a whistle to attract attention in emergency.

Carry map and compass and know how to use them. Recommended maps are Ordnance Survey 1:50,000 sheets 57 and 58, and 1:25,000 NS 89/99 and NN 80/90.

Learn simple first aid, particularly how to recognise if a condition is serious or non life-threatening. Remember that the young and elderly are more susceptible to exposure - which can occur at any time of the year. Carry a small first aid pack.

It is advisable not to go extensively into the hills on your own until you have some experience. Plan your route, tell someone where you are going (maybe a note in your parked car!), and let them know when you return.

It is dangerous to enter shafts or adits of mineral workings unless under competent supervision in a properly equipped party. Minerals and semi-precious stones strictly speaking belong to the owners of the land or mineral rights. Anyone seriously collecting mineral samples should obtain prior permission.

Though footpaths may be indicated or mentioned this does not necessarily mean that they are legal rights of way. Disturbances to farming and forestry must be avoided, observe the Country Code, leave no litter, be responsible and considerate. Dogs must be tightly under control; these are sheep hills.

Learn to read weather signs and obtain information – tel. Weathercall 0891 500 423, Hills – 0891 333 198, and daily papers, radio, TV and Teletext. Do not be complacent about weather conditions. They can change markedly with altitude (see under Climate/Weather), and change very quickly indeed. Be sensible and be prepared to retreat from the hills when conditions deteriorate.

The Countryside Ranger Services will happily advise on safety and other matters – Beam Engine House, Fishcross, tel. (0259) 769999 and Beechwood House, St. Ninians Road, Stirling tel. (0786) 479000. Mountaineering Club and Mountain Rescue people are happy to advise and often have display and advice centres at local events.

In emergency telephone 999, give full information and location, and stay by that telephone until Police or Mountain Rescue arrive or advise otherwise.

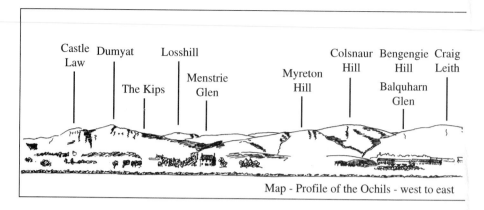

Castle Law, Dumyat, Losshill, The Kips, Menstrie Glen, Myreton Hill, Colsnaur Hill, Bengengie Hill, Balquharn Glen, Craig Leith

Map - Profile of the Ochils - west to east

2 THE OCHIL RANGE

Geology

The Ochils consist of a bed of volcanic rock in the form of a high plateau with a steep southern face. The Ochil Fault, a major geological fault, separates the lavas, e.g – agglomerates and tuffs of the hill mass, from the carboniferous rocks of the Clackmannan Syncline to the south – a syncline is a depression or subsiding trough. The hills are of truncated anticlined form i.e. the rocks are folded in arch form. The Fault is a break in this rock formation creating the sharp drop of the south face of the range and caused by relative movement of strata on either side of the break. This occurred some three hundred and forty million years ago.

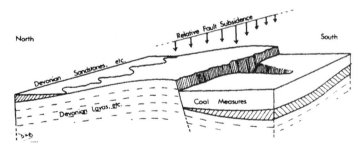
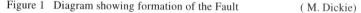

Figure 1   Diagram showing formation of the Fault   (M. Dickie)

The last Ice Age was some ten thousand years ago when the thickness of the ice sheet at its maximum probably covered the tops of the Ochils. When this mass melted, carrying morainic material, boulder clay and gravel, it sculptured and eroded the glens through which it cascaded, and deposited much of its sand and gravel on the lower ground and all the way to the North Sea.

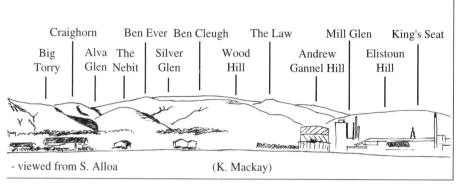

Craighorn Ben Ever Ben Cleugh The Law Mill Glen King's Seat

Big Alva The Silver Wood Andrew Elistoun
Torry Glen Nebit Glen Hill Gannel Hill Hill

- viewed from S. Alloa (K. Mackay)

The Ochils, Comrie/Menstrie line, has a recent history of low seismicity earthquake swarms, latest 1979 and 1969, and records back to 1789.

Characteristics

The unique characteristic of the Ochils lies in the contrast between the north's rolling braes and smooth grassy ridges, and the south where, in consequence of the Ochil geological fault, the hills drop steeply some 600 metres to the plain of the Forth. The result is a spectacular precipitous south face some 20 kilometres long behind the Hillfoot towns and villages. The range extends diagonally across the country from Dunblane to Newburgh on the Tay and may be defined as a line through Greenloaning, Blackford and Glenfarg to the north, and to the south Dunblane, Bridge of Allan, Logie, Dollar and Milnathort; we have presently, however, focused most attention on the area west of Glendevon.

The significant appeal of the hills is their dramatic changes in appearance as sunlight and cloud shadows play on the contours; steep glens contrast with gentle slopes; and the woodland, rock, gorse and bracken add characteristic colour and variety to the ever changing scene.

> "How could a man forget these grassy heights,
>
> Autumn bronzed bracken, the uplifted miles,
>
> the wonder of the vision from their tops.....?"
>
> W.K. Holmes

From west to east the main hills of the range are –

Hill	feet/metres	Location	Grid Reference
Dumyat	1376/420	Blairlogie/Menstrie	NS836977
Loss	1363/416	North of Lossburn Reservoir	NS833000
Myreton	1240/378	East of Menstrie	NS858979
Colsnaur	1832/559	North of Balquharn	NS861993
*Blairdenon	2073/631	East of Sheriffmuir	NS866018
Craigleith	1682/513	Alva	NS873983

Torry is the hill forming the eastern shoulder of Craigleith between Carnaughton and Alva Glens.

Ben Gengie	1853/565	North of Alva	NS869002
The Nebbit	1437/438	Alva	NS888985
Craighorn	1903/580	North of Alva	NS884002
*Ben Ever	2041/622	North west of Tillicoultry	NS893001
Woodhill	1723/525	East of Alva	NS900985
*Ben Cleuch	2363/721	North west of Tillicoultry	NS903006
*The Law	2094/639	North of Tillicoultry	NS910997
Kirk Craigs	1259/384	Tillicoultry	NS918983
*Andrew Gannel	2198/670	North of Tillicoultry	NS918006
*Kings Seat	2111/644	Harviestoun	NS936998
*Tarmangie	2117/645	North west of Dollar	NS842014
*White Wisp	2110/643	North of Dollar	NS955014
*Innerdownie	2004/611	North west of Glenquey Reservoir	NS967031

*Hillwalking people speak of the Donalds (peaks of between 2000 and 2500 feet in the Lowlands catalogued for the Scottish Mountaineering Club by Percy Donald), and of "Doing the Round of Nine".

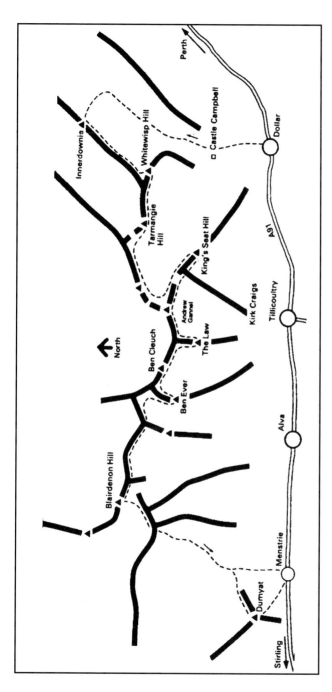

Figure 2 - The 'Round of 'Nine' - the Donalds, 2000-2500ft hills   (R.McOwan in *Wild Walks*)

Heaven keep the Ochil rampart free,
    That rises green amang us!
What better randyvoo could be,
    If fate or folly dang us?
May never tunnel pierce its hert,
    Nor mill nor mine disturb it,
But Nature flourish here, and Airt
    Keep in her Lowland orbit.

Ae moodiewart there was that socht   (a mole
    To mine an' mak' a gain o't;
Thank Heaven! his howkin' cam' to nocht,
    He'd naething but the pain o't.
But had that limmer ha'en the power–
    We ken what bizz'd in he's caip!
He'd whummled the haill Ochils ower
    As I would cowp a beeskep!
But what does impious Folly care
    For happy habitations?
She'd overturn a palace fair
    To seize on the foundations.

Hugh Haliburton
Ochil Idylls and other Poems, 1891

3 MINERALS AND ROCKS

Minerals

Many mineral veins are connected with the Ochil Fault but they are not generally of high quality. There has been much trial work searching for minerals, some optimistically inspired by the mysterious short-lived period of astonishing profitability around 1714 in the Silver Glen at Alva. However cobalt was mined with some success after the silver mines ceased to produce, and copper from the Bridge of Allan mines had earlier supplied the Scottish Mint. The following will serve as a quick reference to some of the minerals and where they have been found.

Minerals	Location	Remarks
Silver	Mainly Silver Glen at Alva but also some amounts at Carnaughton Glen (Alva), Airthrey, Blairlogie, Daiglen (Tillicoultry) and Dollar	It is said that Sir John Erskine of Alva had a yield of £4,000 per week at the height of production at the Silver Glen – an enormous amount of money in the 1712-1715 era.
Copper	Mainly at Bridge of Allan, Tillicoultry and Dollar but smaller amounts at Airthrey, Blairlogie, Balquharn and Jerah (north of Dumyat)	It is said that the first coinage of the 'bawbee' was struck from Bridge of Allan copper at the mint in Stirling at the time of the Coronation of Queen Mary in 1543 and that the last striking of that coin was also of Bridge of Allan copper in 1697.
Cobalt	Mainly at Silver Glen but smaller amounts at Daiglen	Cobalt from the Silver Glen was sold mainly to the pottery industry at Prestonpans to give a blue colouring to their products.
Iron	Airthrey, Blairlogie and Balquharn	In very small quantities.
Lead	Blairlogie and Dollar	In very small quantities.
Calcite	Menstrie	Mined in Napoleonic times on Myreton Hill.

Figure 3
One of a pair of Alva communion cups (ex argento indigena)
presented to the parish church in 1767 by Lord Alva

(R. Snaddon)

Semi Precious Stones

These have been found in the Ochils in a band extending from Blairlogie to Dollar at altitudes between 60m and 200m.

Since some people enjoy collecting such stones and maybe cutting and polishing them the following is a brief list.

Material	Remarks
Quartz	Most common is white quartz. This can be found in most of the veins in the area and also as large loose lumps in the glacial till. Varieties other than white may be found in the Ochils – smokey, citrine (yellow), sard (brown), plase (green), plasma (green) and bloodstone (red and green).
Amethyst	Found as beautiful crystals lining geodes in the rocks cut through by the Balquharn Burn, it is a very delicate shade of purple, tending towards blue at the base.
Agate	Mostly rather pale in colour; some with concentric rings. Easily identified by their green coating when found in the native rock or by their 'toad'-like skin when they have been tumbled in the burn. Agates can be found in most of the glens and burns. The best areas are Balquharn Glen, Kirkcraigs and the Myreton.
Onyx	A black and white banded stone found in the western part of the area.
Jasper	One of the commonest minerals found in the Ochils, occurs on the face of Myreton Hill and at the Silver Mine at Airthrey. Jasper is nearly always red or brown in the Ochils.

An individual pebble may be compounded of one or more of such materials.

Quarries

Quartz, quartz dolerite or whinstone is worked at Tillicoultry. Mainly used for road metal and sometimes for concrete aggregate. It was also quarried at Dollar.

Diorite was worked around the early 19th century for road metal. It is inferior for that purpose to the quartz dolarite which is now generally used.

Andesite and basalt like quartz dolarite is quarried at Tillicoultry.

Basalt Dyke used to be quarried at Alva, also for road metal

NB The Fort was above the quarry

Figure 4 Pictish Fort (RCAHM) and quarry – The Ochils 'gash', Castle Craig, Tillicoultry

4 CLIMATE/WEATHER

The Ochil Hills have an environment characteristically cool, wet and windy, making for rather inhospitable conditions for both plants and animals. The steepness of the range of climatic deterioration with altitude, here and in much of Scotland, contributes towards the strong differentiation between highland and lowland.

Sun in the hills is affected by cloud conditions and topography with a dramatic variety of lighting and heating effects. Generally hills have more cloud cover which reflects, absorbs and scatters sunlight resulting in less solar heating than the adjacent valleys and lowlands except on cloudless days, when the uplands cleaner hill air might add a little warmth.

15

Air temperature decreases with altitude, the commonly used rate being 0.5 degrees C per 100m, but for the Ochils is 0.79°C. Average rates of change are much steeper during the day (1.14°C) than during the night (0.44°C). Indeed, because of the accumulation of dense cold air over low lying ground, hills are frequently warmer during the night, especially in autumn. The effects of altitude on temperature are also greater during spring and summer hence noticeably reducing the length of the growing season, estimated at 16 weeks a year over much of the Ochils, in contrast to more than 23 weeks over the Forth lowlands. Similarly soil temperatures decrease with altitude.

Winds are strongly influenced by altitude and topography e.g. a fresh breeze in Stirling (10 m/s) could be a gale (20m/s) on Ben Cleuch at 720 m.

Relative humidity also increases with altitude particularly in daytime e.g. 90% over the Forth Valley may reach 100% at 650m resulting in a capping of low cloud. Such clouds are major contributors of atmospheric pollution on higher ground.

Precipitation on the Ochils is mainly from Atlantic low pressure systems and their associated fronts and again increases with altitude (see data below). On snow an estimated one extra day for every 7.5 m may apply.

Stirling's annual ten days could exceed sixty over much of the Ochils.

Temperature and Precipitation Annual Averages –

	Stirling (Parkhead) 35m 1971-1989	Ochils (Carim) 332m 1981-1989
Max. Temp.°C	12.4	8.9
Min. Temp.°C	4.8	3.5
Soil Temp.°C at 3cm	9.2	NA
Total Precipitation	922.2	1512

Annual Climatological Bulletins by the Environmental Science Department at Stirling University have been published since 1980 in the *Forth Naturalist and Historian* describing the weather month by month and tabulating data on temperatures, rainfall etc; in Volume 5 1980 is a paper by Harrison on rainfall in the area back to the 1860s, and in volume 16 1993 he reviews the weather over the last 25 years.

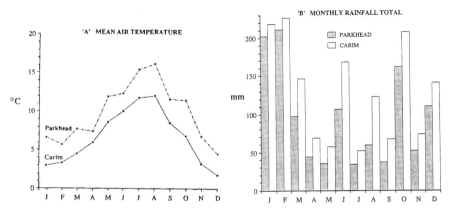

Figure 5 - Altitude effects: temperature and precipitation 1990 - J. Harrison

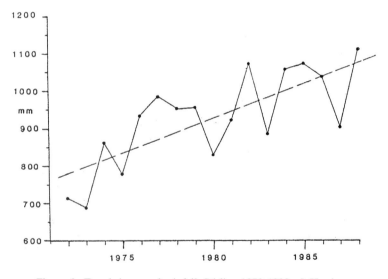

Figure 6 - Trends in annual rainfall, Stirling 1972-1988 - J. Harrison

5 THE WATERS

Following the Ice Age (p8 above) water courses on the hills as we know them today were established or consolidated, and in some places the land was formed to what came to be a convenient configuration for catchments and reservoirs. Glendevon is such and has five reservoirs within a few miles.

The principle reservoirs and their locations are –

Cocksburn	Bridge of Allan
Lossburn	Menstrie
Upper Glendevon (new Frandy)	Glendevon
Lower Glendevon (old Frandy)	Glendevon
Sherup	Glendevon
Glenquey	Glendevon
Castle Hill (Dun Law)	Glendevon
Glenfarg	Glenfarg

Figure 7 - Castle Hill dam and reservoir (R. Snaddon)

On occasion water (as water spouts, not just hilltop saturation) may have been responsible for catastrophes like the great flood of 1877 (Gibson 1883 and *Stirling Journal* 31/8 1877 4C), but normally the many burns, dams and rivers of the Ochils provide drainage and essential water supplies and enhance the scenic attractions of the hills.

Peat moss on the hilltops described by Beveridge (1888) as "delightfully elastic and velvety to the tread", and McOwan (1988) "the moss, a series of peat hags and rough moorland, a bit of highland scenery set down on the lowland hills", was once more extensive and made hard going of crossing the hills. Gibson says that mid 19th century extensive drainage e.g. the wide drains on Helen's Muir behind Tillicoultry, resulted in quicker run-off from the hills. The steadier flow of the burns in earlier times, before steam and electricity, had provided the substantial power for the thriving woollen industry of the Hillfoot towns.

Listen to the burn...

Rippling and gurgling it
Twists and turns,
pouring out in amber flow
its story of the melting snow
and rushing on to roaring falls
it tells of other, softer, calls

Listen to the burn...

It loves to drift,
loosely and soothingly in
summer-haze, with all swiftness
gone, and an urge to laze and
dream of further
golden days.

Listen to the burn...

Chuckling, it tells of hidden
life, of wind-borne flowers ablaze
with light, of glistening rocks
and spray-soaked leaves, all lost,
yet still perceived
by peaceful eyes.

Listen to the burn of many voices,
it talks of joy and rest and solace.

Rennie McOwan

Figure 8 - The Burn

Whyles owre a linn the burnie plays,

As thro' the glen it wimpl't,

Whyles round a rocky scaur it strays,

Whyles in a wiel it dimpli't;...   Robert Burns

The following are some of the burns that give so much pleasure to walkers, and to anglers fishing for the sweet tasting trout –

Wharry	Sheriffmuir
Menstrie	Menstrie Glen
Balquharn	Balquharn Glen
Alva	Alva Glen
Winnel	Behind Nebbit Hill
Tillicoultry	Mill Glen (Tillicoultry)
Daiglen	Off Mill Glen
Gannel	Off Mill Glen
Dollar	Dollar Glen
Sorrow	Off Dollar burn
Care	Off Dollar burn

With few exceptions, for example the North and South Queich burns, the waters leaving the hills all flow eventually into the Forth.

Rivers

The Allan Water rises to the north of the hills in Strathallan, flows round the west end by Dunblane and Bridge of Allan on its way south to join the Forth before Stirling.

The Devon rises at an altitude of 565 m in the hills of Glendevon flowing east then south round the Crook of Devon, then westwards along the Hillfoots south of the urban developments and into the Forth at Cambus. (In pre-glacial times it flowed only eastwards into Loch Leven!). The Black Devon is part outwith our area to the south.

Note that although these two rivers the Allan and the Devon start by flowing in entirely opposite directions, they enter the windings of the Forth within a few miles of one another.

Hoo sweet their watters to the e'e,
  Or round the ankles playin',
Or mairried to the barley-bree,
  The fisher's thirst allayin'!
Gang freely, fishers, by their banks,
  Baith foreign loons an' locals,
An' fill your creels, an' breathe your thanks,
  That Nature made the Ochils!

Wha wadna keep this rampart free,
  That rises green amang us?
What ither haunt or howff hae we
  When warld's cares owregang us?
It's something to escape the stoor
  The fecht wi' fortune raises,
An' rin a laddie for an hoor
  Barefit amang the daisies.
But here – streek oot your shanks at lairge;
  There's no' a buird to stay ye;
Nor menace o' a trespass chairge,
  Nor upstart to nay-say ye.
There's no' a biggin' wi' a ruif,
  But mak's ye welcome hither;
There's no a farmer wi' a luif,
  But grips ye like a brither.

Hugh Haliburton
Ochil Idylls and other Poems, 1891

6 MAMMALS AND FISH

Mammals

An interesting variety of animals exists on the Ochils. Many are shy creatures and best observed either very early in the morning or during the evening. Patient observation and the following of tracks on soft ground will sometimes be rewarded by sightings. Droppings, telltale burrows, channels or runways are helpful indicators of particular animals.

Although not 'large' in comparative terms, the Roe Deer is the largest of the animals on the Ochils. They favour wooded areas, are not all that numerous and do not congregate in large herds but in small family groups. In early morning or in the evening they may be seen emerging from the woodland to graze. Should you come across a newborn Roe Deer calf in May or early June do resist the temptation to touch. The great naturalist David Stephen (1989, p87) said "the Golden Rule is – leave all young wildlife alone." The only protection these beautiful little animals have is the camouflage of their coat and their ability to lie absolutely still and silent in the undergrowth.

Figure 9 - Roe Deer

Figure 10 - Mountain Hare

On the heather hags above the tree line the Mountain Hare may be seen.

In wooded areas the Grey Squirrel introduced from America is common and has largely ousted the native Red Squirrel, though the reverse is the case north of the Ochils where Red predominate.

Voles are present in large numbers. These little creatures weighing less than an ounce are far more numerous in summer than in winter. They have a lifespan of about one year. Apart from doing some slight damage to pine trees the Vole is harmless. In fact its labours in making runways in the ground assist land drainage. Vole populations have a cyclic pattern of around four years, sometimes with a 'plague' at a peak (Stephen

1989 p 153). In this area there was such a dramatic population explosion in 1957. Numbers per acre are now the normal of some hundreds in summer reducing to a few dozen in winter. They are typically associated with rough ungrazed areas of coarse grass land. The more common is the Short Tailed Vole, though the Bank Vole is also widespread. The latter have caused damage to young trees by ring barking.

Nature provides and in the natural system, Voles are part of the diet of Stoat, Weasel, Fox and Kestrel, all present on the Ochils. Stoat and Weasel may be seen scurrying around the drystane dykes which crisscross the hills and will willingly make a meal of Voles or Wood Mice.

Figure 11 - Stoat   Figure 12 - Pipistrelle

Stoats change colour to become completely white in winter except for the black tip of the tail.

The Shrew and the Vole are found where the soil is deeper and richer.

The Fox is fairly widespread. Their main sources of food are Voles and Wood Mice. They are unpopular with hill sheep farmers at lambing time. However, some people believe they are not always as "black as they are painted". They also eat brambles and other berries and given the chance will relish a bird.

The Rabbit is again much in evidence after the ravages of myxomatosis some years ago – it is a source of food for Stoat, Weasel and Fox.

The Hedgehog is fairly widespread. Though they can be seen during the hours of daylight they are most active after dark. Unfortunately their ability to roll themselves into a ball is no protection against the motor car and many meet their fate crossing the roads. The fully grown Hedgehog is about 24 cm long and has a pointed snout and a small mouth. Though classified as an 'insectivore' it eats worms, birds eggs and small animals. It hibernates in winter.

Bats are present in or about the hills. The most common variety, the tiny Pipistrelle, can often be seen in flight in the evening sky.

The Ochils area of the 1:100,000 (c ⁵/₈" to the mile) map of Centra

Scotland by Bartholomew for Central Regional Council, 1982

Fish

Trout is the predominant fish of the waters of the Ochils, the Burn or Brown being the native species. Man has introduced some Rainbow Trout into certain reservoirs in modern times. These have a fast growth rate and attain greater size and weight than the others. Many people agree that from angling and tasting points of view the native is superior.

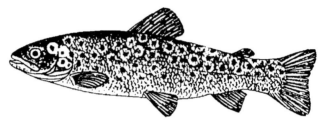

Figure 13 - The Brown Trout

A few Eels and Minnows exist in some reservoirs.

7 BIRDS

Throughout the year about 150 species of birds are present on or around the Ochils. Numbers depend upon the type and the environment in any particular area. The following lists give a general indication of the bird population –

Reservoir River and Burn Based Birds

Arctic Tern	Grey Wagtail	Pied Wagtail
Common Sandpiper	Greylag Goose	Pink Footed Goose
Common Tern	Heron	Pochard
Dipper	Little Grebe	Teal
Golden Eye	Mallard	Tufted Duck
Goosander	Merganser	Whooper Swan
Great Crested Grebe	Mute Swan	Widgeon

The Common Sandpiper and Mallard are the most common of these, while Teal, Goosander and Whooper Swan are not so often seen. Dipper, Heron and Wagtail favour the burns. Widgeon, Golden Eye, Greylag Goose and Whooper Swan are winter visitors only.

Figure 14 - Great Crested Grebe   Figure 15 - Dipper

Woodland Birds

These are found mainly in Redcar Wood – Menstrie, Woodhill – Alva and in the glens.

Black Grouse
Blackcap
Brambling
Bullfinch
Buzzard
Chaffinch
Chiffchaff
Collared Dove
Dunnock
Garden Warbler

Goldcrest
Goldfinch
Greenfinch
Red Grouse
Redpoll
Redstart
Siskin
Sparrow Hawk
Spotted Flycatcher
Stock Dove

Linnet
Tree Pippit
Tree Sparrow
White Throat
Willow Warbler
Woodcock
Wood Pigeon
Wood Warbler

Figure 16 - Spotted Flycatcher   Figure 17 - Buzzard

Tree Sparrows are not too common. The Brambling is a winter visitor only.

Birds – General

Blackbird
Blackheaded Gull
Bluetit
Carrion Crow
Coaltit
Common Gull
Coot
Cuckoo
Curlew
Field Fair
Golden Plover
Greater Black-
 Backed Gull
Greater Spotted-
 Woodpecker
Great Tit
Green Woodpecker
House Martin
House Sparrow

Jackdaw
Jay
Kestrel
Lapwing
Lesser Black-
 Backed Gull
Long-Eared Owl
Long-Tailed Tit
Magpie
Meadow Pippet
Merlin
Mistle Thrush
Moorehen
Oystercatcher
Partridge
Peregrine Falcon
Pheasant
Redshank
Redwing

Reed Bunting
Ring Ouzel
Robin
Rook
Sandmartin
Sedge Warbler
Short-Eared Owl
Skylark
Snipe
Snow Bunting
Song Thrush
Starling
Stonechat
Swallow
Swift
Tree Creeper
Wheatear
Whinchat
Wren
Yellowhammer

Figure 18 - Curlew   Figure 19 - Wheatear

Yellowhammers frequent farm land (they call "a little bit of bread and no cheese"). The Meadow Pippit is very common. Cuckoos like to lay their eggs in Meadow Pippit nests. Magpie, Tree Creeper, Jay and all the Tits are fond of glens. Chiffchaff, Goldcrest, Sedge Warbler, Spotted Flycatcher, Stonechat, Swallows, Wheatear, Whinchat, and Willow Warbler are all summer visitors.

Fieldfare, Redwing and Snow Bunting are winter visitors.

Golden Plover when seen are on the high hilltops. The Green Woodpecker calls "yack, yack, yack" repeating from three to eight times.

Kestrels nest in the crags and gullies and hover above the hilltops.

Figure 20 - Green Woodpecker   Figure 21 - Kestrel

Short-Eared Owls are the only Owls normally seen hunting in daylight and most likely seen between Glenquey and Glendevon. They are not at all numerous.

In addition to the above there have been a few sightings of the Golden Eagle. These spectacular birds are in many ways similar in appearance to Buzzards but the Eagle is much larger, the 'fingers' on the wingtips more pronounced, and of course is rarely seen.

Note that annual Bird Reports of Central Scotland are published in the *Forth Naturalist and Historian*.

8 INSECTS

Butterflies and Moths

The Ochils is an especially rich area for Butterflies with at least 15 different species and there are hundreds of species of Moths. Some Butterflies are widespread and have a range of habitats – Small White, Large White, Small Tortoiseshell and Small Heath frequent open grassland, woods and gardens. Others though quite common have preferred habitats – Meadow Brown and Small Copper – rough ground and wasteland; Green-Veined White only in damp or boggy fields in spring, though more wide ranging in summer; Common Blue only where its food plant, Birdsfoot Trefoil is common.

Figure 22 - Large White

Figure 23 - Meadow Brown

Three species are immigrants though not regular – Red Admiral appears most years, Painted Lady and Peacock more sporadically.

Other species that can be seen are extremely local. The Green Hairstreak is well camouflaged and rarely noticed but found at higher levels in spring swarms on Blaeberry moors; the Dark Green Fritillary in wilder parts of the upper hills; the Ringlet and Small Pearl-Bordered Fritillary form a few colonies in marshland.

One of the most interesting Ochils butterflies is the Scotch Brown Argus, found on the sunny south-facing slopes since early last century and still seen where Rockrose grows. Usually a coastal Butterfly in Scotland its presence here and that of several Moths, for example the Six Spot Burnet, is an indication of a maritime element in the fauna.

Figure 24 - Scotch Brown Argus

Figure 25 - Six Spot Burnet

Other Insects

The Grasshopper although not the easiest of insects to see, is plentiful. Its presence is indicated by the chirping of the males to attract mates. The sound is made by the rubbing of the hind legs across ridges on the wing. Small pegs of the legs strike the veins setting up vibrations.

Figure 26 - Grasshopper   Figure 27 - Dragonfly

Bees and Wasps buzz around the flowers in search of nectar and create one of the most pleasant of summer sounds.

Ants build their nests under stones where it is cool and moist.

Male St. Mark's Flies may be seen on summer days flying up and down looking for females sitting in the grass below.

Dragonflies, Waterboatmen, Whirlygig and Great Diving Beetles inhabit many of the waters.

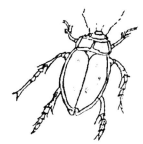 

Figure 28 - Great Diving Beetle   Figure 29 - Ladybird

Hoverflies, Ladybirds and many more insects can be seen but the above may be sufficient to draw attention to this fascinating subject.

9 FLORA

The Ochils may be described as upland acid grassland. The plant list extends beyond 200 different species; only a few are mentioned here.

Prior to the influx of man, trees covered much of the land. Trees were felled for firewood, timber uses and agricultural reasons. By the 16th century it is probable that many of the old forests had gone and domestic animals were grazing the land inhibiting the return of trees.

This had a profound effect on the nature, variety, distribution and numbers of growing plants. Initially the flora would be silvan (woodland based) or bog type; today we have an interesting diversity of plants to enjoy on the hills.

Figure 30 - Gorse

Woodland areas and wetland still exist with their own distinctive flora, e.g. Bluebell. The Whin (Gorse) can be seen in profusion in some areas but sheep grazing limits the growth of this lovely yellow flowering plant which shows such a blaze of colour in summer.

It even grows on loose scree slopes and gives cover for many birds. It also gives the shelter which seedlings and young trees need in order to become established e.g. Hawthorn, Elder, Ash, Bramble, Wild Rose.

When walking in the hills it may appear at first glance that only rough grass is underfoot. However a closer look will reveal a wide variety of flowering plants and grasses. In one place it will be the Wavy Hair-Grass growing in dense tufts, in another the finer feathery-headed Fescue growing on richer soil, also the Crested Hair-Grass and some three dozen others. Those found in the drier areas are Bell Heather, Ladies Bedstraw, Tormentil, Common and Sheeps Sorrel, White Clover, Meadow and Creeping Buttercup, Ladies Mantle, and Yarrow.

Figure 31 - Bell Heather

Figure 32 - Tormentil

The purple flowers of Wild Thyme give a glorious show right through the summer and its scent is a joy to the walker. Bell Heather with its evergreen, purplish foliage and crimson pink flowers adorns some of the hillsides at the height of summer, followed in flowering by the true heather of Scotland – Ling, a plant which is still managed for Grouse moor over some of the northern parts of the Ochils. Associated with heather is the Blaeberry, common on the Ochils.

Where sheep cannot graze in inaccessible rocky outcrops, the pale-yellow flowered Mouse-Eared Hawkweed, Birdsfoot Trefoil and Cat's Ear are to be found, as well as purple Common Knapweed and Harebell, all at their best in late summer. Also in late summer Foxglove provides a beautiful display on some rocky areas as does Wood Sage with a distinctive aroma from its wrinkled leaves when crushed.

Where the hand of man has been at work Thistles, Common Hawkweed, Nettles and Common Ragwort are in evidence. Where the rocks have weathered to soil rich minerals, such plants as Common Rockrose, Dipers Bugloss, Dropwart, Storksbill, Fairy Flax, Autumn Hawkbit and Field Madder may occur.

In wetland areas, Common Butterwort, Sundew, Bog Stitchwort, Bog Asphodel, Marsh Marigold, Water Forget-me-not, Yellow Flag Iris and many other water-related plants may be seen, and in some marshes Ladies Smock (cuckoo flower) and Spearwort.

Figure 33 - Common Butterwort   Figure 34 - Sundew

A word about the preservation of wild growing plants. Please, no matter how tempting, do not uproot them. Indeed the recent Wildlife and Countryside Act makes such an action illegal.

Ferns are worthy of mention and enhance the beauty of the hills in harmony with other growing things. The following are some –

Beech Fern	Common Spleenwort	Lemon Scented Fern
Black Spleenwort	Golden Male Fern	Male Fern
Bladder Fern	Hard Fern	Oak Fern
Bracken	Hard Shield Fern	Parsley Fern
Common Buckler Fern	Harts Tongue	Wall Rue
Common Polypody	Lady Fern	

Of these Bracken is by far the most widespread, covers large areas of hillside and provides good habitat for wildlife, but it can overgrow land required for grazing or other use. It is extremely difficult to eradicate. Its black creeping root system produces shoots each year which develop thick stems with leaflets arranged featherwise. When burnt it is highly alkaline helping to neutralise acids in the soil. It is poisonous and carcinogenic at least to cattle.

Although much of the Ochils is devoid of trees there are areas of both native and alien species, mostly in glens. Woodhill on the south face of the range east of Alva and Red Carr Wood at the foot of Dumyat to the west of Menstrie, are good examples of areas returning to their original wooded state after felling. Red Carr Wood contains Sycamore, Oak, Ash, and Elm, Sycamore being predominant. Spruce, Larch and Scots Pine are also present. The once plentiful Oak is now much diminished but there is some in Red Carr Wood and Balquharn Glen. Elm, Sycamore, Beech and Chestnut are to be found in the Ochil Hills Woodland Park to the east of Alva.

A few commercial conifer plantations are perhaps less desirable features of the landscape.

The following are some of the trees of the Ochils –

Alder	Gean	Rowan
Ash	Horse Chestnut	Scots Pine
Beech	Larch	Spruce
Birch	Norway Maple	Sweet Chestnut
Elm		Oak Sycamore

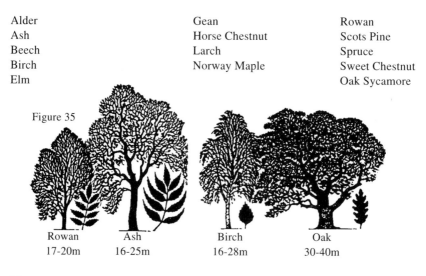

Figure 35

Rowan	Ash	Birch	Oak
17-20m	16-25m	16-28m	30-40m

10 THE BATTLES

The sites of several battlefields may be viewed from the Ochils e.g. Stirling Bridge, Bannockburn, Sauchieburn. Battles actually fought on the hills include Dumyat (c 570 AD) when Aidan King of the Scots of Dalriada defeated the Pictish King Brude – a significant victory indicating the rising power of the Scots. Some three hundred years later, Constantine I, son of MacAlpine defeated the invading Danes at Dollar. The most recorded however is the Battle of Sheriffmuir. In 1715 the forces of the ruling establishment faced the Jacobite army of The Old Pretender, James II (VII of Scotland). The ensuing battle, though indecisive, ended any hope of success for the Rising.

The Clan MacRae who fought on the Jacobite side have erected a monument to their dead near the site of the battle on the gentle slopes above Dunblane. The Commander-in-Chief of the Jacobite forces, John 6th Earl of Mar, had previously been much in favour with Queen Anne. In 1705 he was appointed Secretary of State for Scotland and in the following year made a Knight of the Thistle. He is noted also for his work in helping to bring about the union of the Scottish and English parliaments although many in Scotland did not approve of such a union. However, Queen Anne died in 1714 and George, Elector of Hanover, ascended the throne; straight away Mar was dismissed from the office of Secretary of State and stripped of his governership of Stirling Castle – which drove the Alloa laird straight into the arms of the Jacobite cause.

Figure 36 - The MacRae Monument   Figure 37 - Jacobite Soldier

By mid-September 1715 Mar was commissioned by James as Commander-in-Chief of all his forces in Scotland. Two months later on 13th November, he found himself with the Jacobite army facing the government forces on the Ochils at Sheriffmuir. The battle was inconclusive. The Jacobite 'left of the line' seems to have been routed and fled pursued by the troops opposing them, whilst the Jacobite right triumphed over the left and centre of the enemy, but failed to press home their advantage. An old ballad sums it up –

There's some say that we wan,
Some say that they wan,
Some say that nane wan at a' man!
But ae thing I'm sure,
That at Sherra-muir,
A battle there was a' saw man,
And we ran, and they ran,
And they ran, and we ran,

And we ran, and they ran awa' man

Figure 38 - Redcoat Foot-soldier

The pursuit of the defeated left of the Jacobite army fizzled out, the remainder staying where they were and the Hanovarians filtered down the hill to Dunblane. As night approached Mar marched his forces back a couple of miles from the field of battle to obtain shelter and provision – the previous night they had lain on the open moors without supplies. Come the morning Mar found he was left with but a small number of men, the bulk of the Highlanders having decided to go home.

The failure of the Jacobites to secure a conclusive victory at Sheriffmuir caused James to leave Scotland, though not before he had created John Earl of Mar a Duke, and bestowed other favours upon him. Mar fled the country never again to return and his estate was forfeit to the crown. He died in Aix-La-Chapelle in 1732 after a number of years in poor health.

Among others who suffered for supporting the Jacobite cause was Sir John Erskine of Alva. Lady Erskine and her helpers at Alva House cared for many wounded after the battle. She was an avid Jacobite, employing spies to obtain intelligence for the cause. On the day of the battle, the local minister is said to have sent a message to Alva House: "There wad be nae sabbath the day" and the kirk bell was silent. Many guid folk had gone to watch the goings-on at Sheriffmuir: no doubt from a respectable distance.

Like the Earl of Mar, Sir John Erskine was obliged to slip away overseas but, unlike Mar, he was able to return later by an arrangement for the procurement of silver from his mines at Alva.

Mar   Erskine

Figure 39: After the Battle

11 FORTIFICATIONS AND CASTLES

Fortifications

The Picts had several forts on the hills. An Iron Age fort once stood on the side of Dumyat to the west of the summit. An old spelling is Dun Myat. Dun indicates a fortified position, Myat is derived from the Maeatae or 'people of the plain', the Gaelic 'mach' meaning a plain.

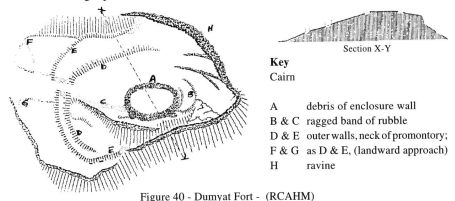

Section X-Y

Key

Cairn

A   debris of enclosure wall
B & C ragged band of rubble
D & E outer walls, neck of promontory;
F & G as D & E, (landward approach)
H   ravine

Figure 40 - Dumyat Fort - (RCAHM)

Another Pictish fort once stood on the summit of Castle Craig at Tillicoultry (see at Figure 4) but little now remains to indicate its existence. It would have been protected to the south and east by precipitous cliffs, and traces of a ditch and ramparts protecting other approaches may still be seen. A similar fort once stood at the entrance to

Glendevon. These were part of a chain of forts across the country which could signal to one another by bonfires. They were of the characteristic Pictish type known as 'nuclear' forts built on craggy sites consisting of stretches of ramparts linking natural defences such as steep cliffs and natural ditches. An arrangement of 'courts' with staggered entrances led to a citadel on the highest point on the hill.

The Romans' great fort at Lundum (Ardoch) was north of the Hills at Braco where soldiers from Rome, Syria, Greece, Spain and other Roman provinces in the 80-200 AD period, paced the high, grassy ramparts and looked out on the surrounding hills – the land of the Picts.

Castles

The main castles are Campbell, Glendevon and Menstrie.

Castle Campbell, in the care of Historic Scotland, stands in lofty isolation upon a narrow eminence over-topped by a crescent of higher hills and has a precipitous ravine on either side. This impressive 15th century fortalice between the burns of Care and Sorrow dominates the wooded Dollar Glen. Both Glen and Castle are the property of the National Trust for Scotland.

By gradual development it achieved its present form during the 15th, 16th and 17th centuries. Of the existing buildings the 60 foot high tower, standing on what was once the motte of a 'motte and bailey' castle, is the oldest, dating from the latter part of the 15th century. The southern enclosure with additional accommodation was 16th century. Later alterations were made to the eastern range so completing the elegant and beautifully proportioned building seen today.

A royal castle in early times, the stronghold came into the possession of the Argyll family in 1481 through a marriage contract between the Campbells and the Stewarts of Lorne.

Regarding the alleged burning of the castle by the MacLeans of Montrose's army in 1645 some historians have been confused. It is true that the lands of Dollar and Muckhart were laid waste but *not* the castle as a prominent Cameron was fostered there, and letters of his describe events of the time. Nine years later, it was attacked and destroyed by fire as evidenced in a letter from General Monk to Cromwell – "we are now come hither where we shall stay some few days for refreshment, some parties of the enemy are abroad in the country and on Monday and Tuesday nights last burnt Castle Campbell a house belonging to the Marquis of Argyll". Whatever the precise date, it then ceased to be the great lowland stronghold it once was.

Castle Campbell as well as its dramatic setting and legends associated with such names as Gloom, Gryfe, Care and Sorrow, has seen some notable visitors.

In 1556 John Knox was invited to stay with the Earl and today the spot 'the pulpit' is pointed out as where he is said to have dispensed communion according to the reformed religion.

1563 saw a three day visit by Mary Queen of Scots when attending the marriage of Sir James Stewart of Doune and Lady Margaret Campbell, daughter of Archibald, fourth Earl of Argyll. Mary was back two years later with her husband Darnley in the course of subduing some rebellion against their marriage.

At Devil's Mill by Rumbling Bridge there is a cave which figures romantically in the 1745 Rising. The hero was Hector MacEachan, a nephew of the Lord Provost of Glasgow, who was arrested on his way to join Prince Charlie's army. While imprisoned at Castle Campbell he was befriended by Hannah Haig of Dollarfield. With her connivance Hector escaped from the castle into hiding at the Devil's Mill, Rumbling Bridge. After the hue and cry had subsided he managed to join the Prince's army, only to end up as one of the Jacobites on trial at Carlisle. He would have shared their fate, as most of them were condemned to death, had there not been some bungling of the evidence. Hannah Haig was in court to hear his acquittal and later the couple were married.

Robert Burns, accompanied by Charlotte Hamilton and his lost love Peggy Chalmers, visited the castle in 1787; and later Sir Walter Scott and friends.

Glendevon Castle, now a restaurant, was a keep built by the Red Douglas, Earl of Angus around the year 1442. It was last used as a fortified building during the 1745 Rising. "Luckless Jacobite prisoners were held in its dungeons before being executed by hanging at Gallows Hill," says a notice there, but we understand no real evidence of this is known.

Figure 41 - Castle Campbell   Figure 42 - Glendevon Castle (RIAS)

Menstrie Castle, the birthplace of Sir William Alexander 1567-1640, first Earl of Stirling and founder of Nova Scotia, also in 1734 of Sir Ralph Abercrombie of Aboukir, is a late 16th century fortified house. It was saved from demolition after the Second World War by the Clackmannanshire Local Authority with the aid of Historic Buildings of Scotland, the Pilgrim Trust and public subscriptions here and in Canada in a campaign led by the actor and conservationist Moultrie R. Kelsall. This picturesque, sturdy, three-storey castellated house converted into flats, now makes the distinguished feature of a small housing estate. It incorporates a commemoration room to the Baronets of Nova Scotia (still awaiting refurbishment), administered by the National Trust for Scotland.

Harviestoun Castle, was 18th century; rebuilt and extended by John Tait, a wealthy Edinburgh lawyer in the early 19th century. It was demolished in the 1970s. Gate lodges, stables and home farm still remain. Here Robert Burns stayed on his highland tour in 1787.

Other Ochils area castles include Cowden, Glen Eagles, Kincardine, Balvaird, while Stirling, Kilbride, Tullibole and Loch Leven are not far distant; and there are tower houses – Blairlogie, Alloa, Sauchie, Clackmannan (Swan 1987, Tranter 1971).

Figure 43 - Menstrie Castle

12 PEOPLE

Before the Romans, the Picts inhabited the Ochils and surrounding countryside. Then invaders from Holland and Germany sailed up the 'Frisian Sea' (Firth of Forth) and took over that part of the Pictish kingdom called Forthreve, including the southern slopes of the Ochils. However the Picts did not let matters rest there and ultimately they overcame these Frisians and re-occupied the land. Thus those mysterious people called Picts had their abode on and around the Ochils for a very long time – were there when the Romans came to Scotland about 70 AD and were still there when they left in the fourth century.

Then came the Scots from Ireland who had settled in the west, the Angles from the south, Britons from what is now south west Scotland, and Danes and Vikings. These, with others more recent e.g. dispossessed highlanders, Irish labourers, Italians and Polish ex-servicemen, have blended together to produce the couthy, careful and often talented people who occupy the Ochils area.

13 NAMES

The following are possible meanings of some of the names referred to. All are thought to be of Gaelic origin unless otherwise indicated.

Airthrey	Steep field or sub-division
Allan	Beautiful or pleasant
Alloa	(Celtic) Rock plain
Alva	As Alloa
Andrew Gannel	Sandy bottomed burn
Ardoch	A high field or place
Argyll	Coast or portion of the Gael
Balqhuarn	Blue rock farm, or Cairn township
Ben Cleuch	Stony peak or slope; ravine or narrow glen
Ben Ever	Granite peak
Ben Gengie	Mount of the tongue
Blairdenon	Battle site or flat place
Blairlogie	Land of the hollow
Braco	Grey place
Cambus	Bay or bend
Carnbo	Rock of the cattle
Colsnaur or Cul Snaur	Cul-back of, snaur-cut down
Craighorn	Blue rock
Craigleith	Grey rock
Craigonish or Craigomas	Craig o' the moss

Devon	Black river
Dollar	(Brittonic) Black or cultivated ground
Doune	Fort or hill
Dumyat	Fort of the Maeatae or Hill of Good Prospect
Dunblane	Hill of Blann (head of monastery c600 AD)
Falkirk	(Old Scots) Dappled or speckled church
Finglen	White glen
Forth	A boundary
Glendevon	Glen of the black river, or deep glen
Glenfarg	Glen of anger or violence
Inchna	Island of the ford
Innerdownie	Mouth of the Downiburn
Kilbride	Sanctuary of St. Bride
Kincardine	(Gaelic/Brittonic) Bend of deep; head of wood
King's Seat	Head seat
Kips	Tufts or tussocks
Kirk Craigs	(Gaelic/Brittonic) Fort of the rocks
Law	A mound or hill
Loch Leven	(Celtic/Brittonic) Flood lake
Logie	A ditch or stream
Loss	Cultivated enclosure
Menstrie	(Brittonic) Hamlet in the plain
Muckhart	Wild boar height
Myreton	(English/Old Scots) Boggy farm township
Ochil	(Brittonic) High
Queich	A cup or hollow land
Sheriffmuir	From siora (long) or (English) Moor of the Sheriff
Stirling	(Brittonic) Dwelling of Velyn, a personal name
Tarmangie	Hill of the fawn or goat
Tillicoultry	Hill behind the land
Torry	Mound or knowl
Tullibody	Hill of the bothy or hut
Tullibole	Hill of danger

14 REFERENCES AND FURTHER READING

Airthrey and Bridge of Allan	Walk and Brief History. 32pp Forth Naturalist and Historian. 1986. ISBN 09506962 6 9.
Ardoch Roman Fort, Braco	A Guide, 1983.
BERNARD, RICHARD	Walks in the Hills, 1984; Devon Valley Diary, 1985; Off the Beaten Track, 1986; Walking the Ochils and Beyond, 1987. Clackmannan District Libraries.
BEVERIDGE, D.	Between the Ochils and the Forth. 318pp. 1888.
BROWN, W.	Clackmannanshire – An Index Guide to Historical Sources. 390 pages. Forth Naturalist and Historian, 1980. op
Central Scotland	Land, Wildlife, People – a new survey by Forth Naturalist and Historian. 332pp. 1993.
Clackmannan District Council	Buildings of Architectural and Historical Interest. 48pp. 1981.
Clackmannanshire District Ranger Service	A programme of guided walks; Countryside Walks; Menstrie to Tillicoultry, Glendevon to Dollar, Tillicoultry to Dollar (the Devon Way), Mill Glen Trail Guide – Tillicoultry.
Clackmannanshire Field Studies Society	Mines and Minerals of the Ochils, 1974, reprint 1986.
Corbetts and other Scottish hills	Scottish Mountaineering Trust. 1990.
DICKIE, D.M.	Cultivation terraces along the Ochils escarpments, *Forth Naturalist and Historian* Vol 1, 123-140. 1976.
Dollar Chap Book	Dollar Civic Trust. 60 pp. 1977.
DORWARD, D.	Scotland's Place Names. 61 pp. 1979.
Exploring Scotland's Heritage	(the Clyde Estuary and Central Region). Royal Commission on Ancient and Historical Monuments of Scotland, 158pp. 1985.
FERGUSSON, MENZIES	Ochil Hills Fairy Tales. 155 pp. (1912) Reprint by Clackmannanshire District Libraries, 1985.
FILLAN	Traditional Stories of the Rebellion of 1745.
The Forth Naturalist and Historian	124 page volumes of articles from 1976 (Vol 16 current) – annual reports on climate and birds; studies research papers on naturalist, environmental and historical subjects; with 5 year indexes.
GIBSON, W.	Reminiscences of Dollar, Tillicoultry and other Districts adjoining the Ochils. 240pp. 1883. Facsimile reprint by Strong Oak Press, 1990. op
The Great Flood 1877	Clackmannan District Libraries. 6 pp. 1981.
HALDANE, A.R.B.	The Drove Roads of Scotland, EUP 1952
HALIBURTON, H.	Ochil Idylls and other Poems. 162pp. 1891.

HOLMES, W.K.	In the Open – verses. 66pp. 1925.
KINNAIRD, H.	Rhymes Frae the Ochils. 28pp. priv. print 1992.
KINROSS, J.	Discovering Scottish Battlefields. 50 pp. Shire.
MacLAGAN, C.	On round castles of the valley of the Forth. *Proceedings of the Society of Antiquaries of Scotland.* First series Vol 9 1874.
McOWAN, R.	The Green Hills – Stories of the Ochils. Clackmannan District Libraries, 1989.
	Lovely Ochils – *Stirling Observer*, 20th July 1988.
	Chapters in *Wild Walks* and *On Foot through History*.
Maps	Central Scotland 1:100,000
	Bartholomew for CRC, 1982.
	Old Ordnance Survey Maps (1890s) – commissioned from Godfrey Maps by Forth Naturalist and Historian. Series of 24 titles including: 4 for Stirling; Bridge of Allan; Alva/Menstrie/Tullibody; Dollar/Muckhart; Tillicoultry.
	OS 1:50,000 sheets 57 and 58.
MOYER, D.G.	Scottish Hill Tracks – Old Highways and Drove Roads. 1988
Muckhart & Glendevon Amenities Soc.	Muckhart – an Illustrated History of the Parish. 98 pp, Forth Naturalist and Historian, 1989.
PARK, B.	Woollen Mill Buildings of the Hillfoots. 180 pp. Forth Naturalist and Historian. 1984.
The Statistical Accounts	Old 1790s, New or second 1835. Third from 1950 – some information in volumes for Clackmannanshire, Stirlingshire and Perthshire parishes; some reprinted by Clackmannan District Libraries.
Stirling Region	The survey for the British Association. 280 pp. 1974. University of Stirling, available from Forth Naturalist and Historian.
SWANN, A.	Clackmannan and the Ochils, illustrated architectural guide. 112 pp. 1987. RIAS.
Walk Loch Lomond and the Trossachs	35 walks by Bartholomew. 1986. Including 10, 11 and 12 Dumyat, Scramble in the Ochils, Ben Cleuch and the Nebbit.
Walk Southern Scotland	Bartholomew – Walk No. 129 Tillicoultry to Blackford or Gleneagles, 9 miles. 1975.

APPENDIX – THREE OCHILS WALKS

WALK 1 – ALVA GLEN Time: about 2 hours.

A not too demanding walk from the Car Park (1)

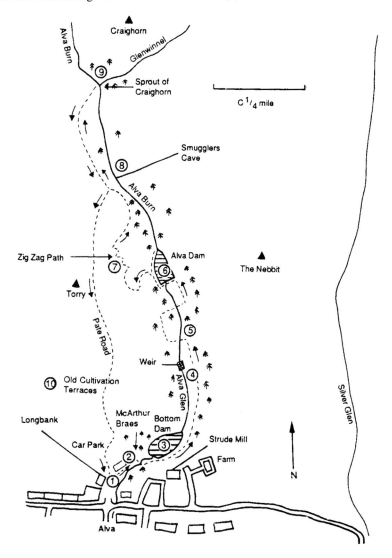

Figure 44 - Alva Glen Walk

On the left, before the car park is Long Bank Works which in the 1880s was a water-powered textile mill. The name derives from long banks, delvins or lynchets where potatoes were grown when first introduced into this part of Scotland at the start of the 19th century. Other buildings around this area were originally mills using the power of the Alva Burn.

The McArthur Braes (2), created as a work project during the 1924 Depression utilise ash bings from the boilers of the Strude mills – now converted to flats. As we walk through the McArthur Braes, we may reflect on their former grandeur when residents and visitors alike spent happy hours strolling through the pleasant gardens beneath tall trees with the burn gurgling by. Bands entertained on fine summer days and for a short time after World War Two 'illuminations' drew large crowds to enjoy the spectacle of fairy lights among the trees, floodlit waters and colourful flower beds.

From the car park follow the path towards the glen passing an old quarry where, it is said, the remains of a dwarf were found. Cross the bridge and bear left to arrive at the viewing point for the falls and dam (3). Here at the bottom of the high cliffs at the entrance to the glen the waters can be impressive, particularly after rain.

Continue upwards by the steps to reach the old cast iron pipe which once fed the Alva mills. At this point we are crossing the Ochil Fault. Behind are the carboniferous (coal bearing) rocks which underlie the Devon Valley and the Carse of the Forth. In front are the lavas, agglomerates (mixtures of lavas and rock fragments) and tuffs (volcanic ash) of the Old Red Sandstone Volcanic Series which make up the Ochil Hills.

Under the pipe turn left. On the right is a waterworks installation and on the left below the path a pipe discharges water down the hillside to the burn below giving a pleasing, if artificial, waterfall effect. The path now cuts into the sheer cliff leading up Alva Glen into the hills. Just through the gate notice that again piped water is giving another waterfall effect.

The path is reasonable but in wet weather can be muddy. Strict supervision of children is necessary particularly for the first part since there is a steep drop from the fence at the side of the path to the burn far below. Here the walk is interesting and diverse as we cross and recross the burn among the trees of the steep sided glen. In places we walk by (or on) the old cast iron water supply pipe which runs down the line of the path. The weir (4), half way up the glen, diverts water into this pipe. Before the bridge a spring on the cliff is known as 'ladies well' (5). Dally here by the bridge – you might see trout in the deep rocky pools.

Proceeding up the glen, the hill to the left is Torry and that to the right the Nebbit. At the head of the glen is the Alva Dam (6) fed by the backfalls and built to provide a reliable source of water for the mills of Alva during the summer. The falls may be viewed from the end of the path alongside the dam. From the dam now take to the steep hillside by the zig zag path (7). Supervision of children is essential not only for their own safety, but to ensure that no loose stones are sent tumbling down the hillside.

Climbing now we pass out of the treeline and can look back down the glen where trees in places grow right to the water's edge or cling tenaciously to the steep slopes. At the top of the zig zag path there is an excellent view down the glen to the country beyond. An iron seat here is a convenient rest point.

Onward again towards Smugglers Cave (8). The first view of this huge cavern through which the burn flows, is from the guard railing on the clifftop. To the left, over some rocks, take the path heading north into the hills – (to explore the Smugglers Cave itself scramble down a rather steep slope). Continue northwards for about ten minutes to a knoll to view the Sprout of Craighorn (9). These falls of the Winnel Burn cascade down from a great height into the Alva Burn.

Returning to the junction above the Smugglers Cave take the path leading over the shoulder of the hill (Torry) towards Alva. These steep grassy slopes can be rather slippery and deaths are on record from falls into the gorge. This path through ancient cultivation terraces (10) is known locally as the 'Pate Road'. These cultivation terraces (the best examples of such on the Ochils) are a series of comparatively flat areas with rubble deposited at the front of each (Dickie 1976). The Pate Road seems to pre-date the terraces since they are discontinuous on either side of the road.

Figure 45 - Alva cultivated terraces with diagonal (Pate Road) path

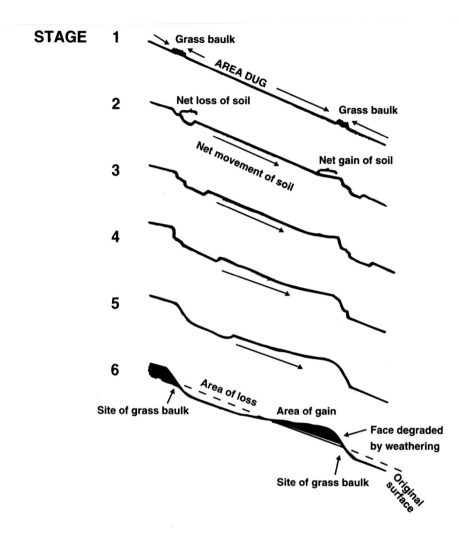

STAGE 1 Grass baulk

AREA DUG

2 Net loss of soil
Grass baulk

Net movement of soil

Net gain of soil

3

4

5

6

Site of grass baulk

Area of loss

Area of gain

Face degraded by weathering

Site of grass baulk

Original surface

Figure 46 - Formation of a cultivation Terrace

The remains of an old stone dyke here once enclosed the common grazing of the village and is believed to have been used until the end of the 17th century. Scrambling down the eroded basalt rocks on the final descent, we recross the line of the Ochil Fault. Over the stile at the east end of the golf course the path leads back into the car park.

WALK 2 – MENSTRIE GLEN

Two main routes are suggested both affording fine views and interesting surroundings. After an initial climb the routes are not too demanding since most of the walking is on fairly flat or undulating hillside. In both cases the Ochil Fault is crossed at the start.

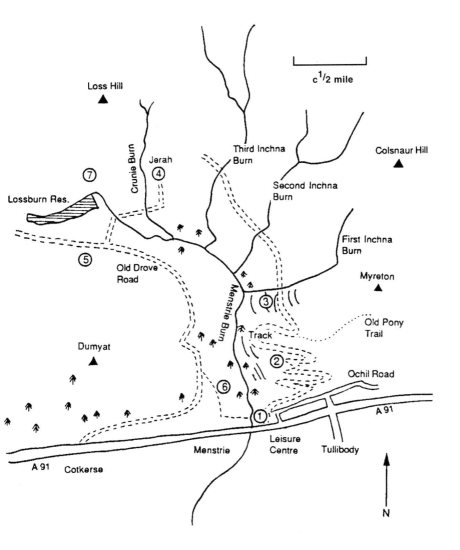

Figure 47 - Menstrie Glen Walks

Menstrie Glen

With pride I view the flock of ewes,
And lambs that sport on Jarah's braes,
Where oft in boyhood I have trod
And pu'd the nuts and glossy slaes.
There have I roam'd when fancy led
My heart to hear the blackbird's strain,
And floods of love spring from the dove
Sweet cooing then in Menstrie Glen.

Yes, there I've roamed and viewed with pride
The flirting, chirping little wren
Gathering food for her young brood,
Sweet nestling in their foggy den.
Yes, those were days of heartfelt glee,
When I was young and doubly fain
To ramble 'mong the blooming whin
And craggy cliffs o'Menstrie Glen.

No more these tardy limbs of mine,
Shall roam those lovely paths again
To ruminate on scenes sublime–
Such as I've viewed in Menstrie Glen.
But still with pride I woo the tide,
That gurgles onward to the main;
It brings to mind my boyish days–
Days that cannot come again.

Robert Jamieson
from *Poets of Clackmannanshire*
J. Beveridge 1885

The East Walk

Time about two hours excluding the Dumyat climb (three hours unrushed if included).

From Main Street, Menstrie (A91), proceed up School Lane opposite the new Leisure Centre to Ochil Road (1). A track zig zagging up the hill can now be seen and is approached by the path and a stile at the west side of a cottage set back from the road. The hill is the Myreton and the shoulder is known as Craigomish or Craigomas. The original track was established as a pony trail when calcite (native crystalised carbonate of lime) was extracted by open cast and adit workings during the Napoleonic Wars. The modern track first roughly follows the line of the original then extends further into the hills towards Jerah Farm and the Lossburn Reservoir. The hillside is grassy with bracken in places. Proceeding up the zig zag (2) examples of agate, quartz and jasper are to be seen. This is one of the best geological walks in the hills.

Views from the top of the zig zag include hills to the west towards Loch Lomond, southwest to the Touch Hills, south to the rising ground beyond the Forth and the Pentlands, Cleish and Lomond Hills to the east.

Beyond Menstrie and the Hillfoots towns in the foreground may be seen the Wallace Monument, Stirling Castle and the windings of the Rivers Forth and Devon. More distant are the towns of Alloa, Falkirk, Stirling; Kincardine Bridge and the power stations of Kincardine and Longannet, Grangemouth and the estuary of the Forth beyond to the southeast.

Another feature which draws the eye is the vast expanse of bonded warehouses at Menstrie, Blackgrange and Cambus. These store much of the grain whisky made in Scotland, maturing before being blended and bottled. The complex first established in 1959 by DCL is the largest of its kind in Scotland – a colossal tax source!

Returning to our walk; we are on Myreton Hill and west across the glen is Dumyat. To the north of Myreton lies Coalsnaur and to the north of Dumyat beyond the Lossburn Reservoir, is Loss Hill. Recognisable examples of early agriculture in the form of cultivation terraces and enclosed fields (3) may be seen either side of the track before crossing the First Inchna Burn.

This path leads over the three Inchna Burns. The first flows from the north side of Myreton Hill; the second flows north to south down the glen to the west of Coalsnaur; the third rises to the north and flows down to join the Menstrie just a bit north west of the other two.

At the first Inchna Burn the view to the northwest is over the Lossburn Reservoir and beyond to the highlands at Callander where Ben Ledi (876m - 2837 ft) stands out against the sky. The track ends near the ruined Jerah Farm (4). Alternatives to retracing one's steps are to descend the hill onto the Jerah track, cross the Menstrie Burn, go round the reservoir and/or join the old drove road (5) southwards along the western side of the Menstrie Glen to return to the village via the 'Kips' (ie the southeastern slopes of Dumyat). The more energetic may decide to climb Dumyat at this point. The ascent from the north is not steep and the view from the summit is well worth the time and effort.

Note : In addition to the calcite mining mentioned above, copper was mined north of the Reservoir probably early in the 18th century. Information concerning these and other mines is given in Clackmannanshire Field Studies Society's booklet *Mines and Minerals of the Ochils*.

The West Walk

Time about two hours if returning by the outward route, or up to three if returning by the east side of the glen.

From the western end of Ochil Road (the old 'back road'), cross the bridge over the burn, turn right at the top of the brae, up the steep tree clad path through a steel gate, then bear left up the path on the hill. The paths to the right lead down towards the burn and are not recommended.

A climb of about 400 yards leads to a fence below the waterworks; crossing the stile (6) the short steep path joins the old drove road leading north up the glen; this part known as the 'Kips' is the southern shoulder of Dumyat. The drove road served as a convenient route for highlanders driving cattle and horses via Sheriffmuir to markets in the carseland and towns to the south. Falkirk for instance, was famous at one time for its horse markets.

The view south from the drove road is similar to that described in the east walk, that to the north looks up the glen with its burn shrouded in trees. These are mainly Witch Elm with some Rowan further away from the burn. The Ash here and on the Ochil Scarp are large compared with other locations in Scotland. A small planting of Sessile Oak on the upper Menstrie Burn is visible from the drove road.

The grassy hillside with its areas of bracken has some ash seedlings here and there but these are rapidly suppressed by animal grazing. This walk along the drove road is pleasant and not at all taxing, perhaps luring the walker into spending more time than was first intended.

Approaching Lossburn Reservoir (7), alternative return routes are to go round the reservoir and/or retrace, or cross the burn at the east end of the reservoir, go up the hillside to the east of old Jerah Farm, and so join the track south to Menstrie as described on the East Walk.

WALK 3 – DOLLAR TO GLENDEVON VIA GLENQUEY Time two to three hours.

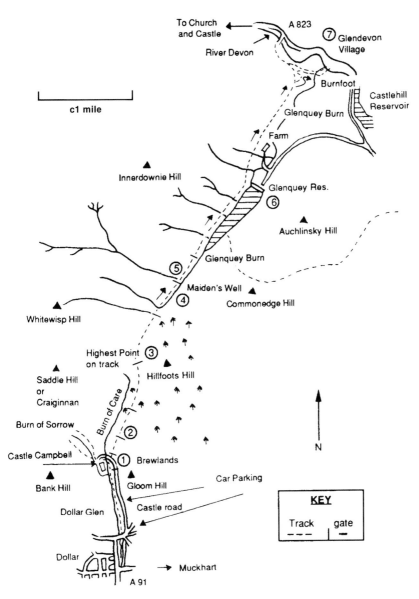

Figure 48 - Dollar - Glendevon Walk

This walk (or its opposite direction) along the route of an old drove road is a favourite with local people and visitors. It requires some prior transport arrangement unless retracked.

An organised car park for accessing Castle Campbell or walks like this one is set out with guide map and notes at Gloom Hill Quarry (P) half way up the castle road from Dollar. From here a short uphill stretch on the road towards Castle Campbell starts our walk. Pausing at the cottage 'Brewlands' (1) with the castle just over the ravine, the view southwards looks down on the National Trust for Scotland owned glen to Dollar, the fertile Devon Valley, and the green land rising beyond. The signpost of our walk now leads us northward (2) beside the Burn of Care then through the conifer plantation. Hereabouts you may detect the telltale musky odour of the Fox and have a slight chance of seeing a Short Eared Owl, not common, but it is said to hunt by day. Leaving the wood by the wall and gate, onto the open hill we are about the highest point on the track 335m (3). Our route is now downhill eastwards alongside the plantation and the stream after fording it where it comes down from White Wisp Hill. Birds are numerous in this glen, particularly Skylarks and Meadow Pippets. Winchats, Wheatears, Curlews, Kestrels and Carrion Crows may be seen, also perhaps Ring Ouzels in summer and Snow Buntings in winter. Occasionally Golden Plover nest on top of White Wisp Hill. The route now is a steep sided glen formed millions of years ago by water from melting ice. Between the track and the small burn and fence on our right watch for a stone and a rather insignificant little pool. This is the Maiden's Well (4) – with a beauty to answer your call, but beware, your life may be forfeit by morning (Dollar Magazine 1904) –

The Spirit of the Maiden's Well   by James Christie

He pass'd the auld grey mossy cairn,
   Whaur heroes mould'ring lie,
And o'er the brae the birken trees
   In safety pass'd he by.

At last he reached the narrow dell,
   But all was silence there –
The voices of the midnight blast
   All sunk and silent were.

Twice he invoked the spirit's name,
   But yet no shape was seen;
Again! the fearful sprite appeared
   In robes of dazzling sheen.

Adown her breast her tresses hung
   In beauty passing fair;
But from her wild and piercing eye
   Flashed passion's kindling glare.

A chill crept Edwin's bosom through,
   He grasped his trusty brand;
But something on his shoulder laid
   Withheld his manly hand.

Again he tried – his strength was gone –
   A lifeless corpse he fell;
And with the victor spirit sunk
   Down in the crystal well.

A short distance on another burn (5) coming from the saddle of White Wisp and Innerdownie to the north is forded as the glen widens out and Glenquey Reservoir is approached offering a view of wooded hills beyond Glendevon. In late spring and early summer admire the delicate blue flower of Butterwort, the deep pink of Lousewort, the yellow of Heartsease and the blue of Scabious. The cry of the Curlew and Lapwing further enhance the scene.

The reservoir (6) is part of the water supply for Fife. Trout fishing permits are available from the council office at Glenrothes. Ducks may be seen on the reservoir – Mallard, Teal, Widgeon, Pochard and Golden Eye. Beyond the dam of the reservoir the track passes to the west of Glenquey Farm. About 600 yards or so beyond the farm the view is north and east to the valley of Glendevon. Downhill a quarter of a mile or so further on the path divides. Take that to the right leading down to the near deserted hamlet of Burnfoot and on to Glendevon village (7) via a footbridge over the river. At the village, the Tormaukin Inn is a pleasant hostelry, it has been there since the old droving days.

As an alternative to retracing the route to Brewlands, if transport has been arranged, the return may be by way of the A823 and Yetts of Muckhart, then the A91 to Dollar and hence Brewlands, a distance of some seven miles. There is a limited bus service with a change at Yetts of Muckart.

An Exile's Thoughts of Home

Far frae the shores o Scotland hae I traivelled,
Across the foamin ocean, wild and wide;
But aye the longin hert keeps turnin, turnin,
Tae that hamestead whaur my parents used tae bide.

It stands upon a braeside o the Ochils,
Wi gowden whin an broom on ilka side;
Bloomin through aa the lang, fair simmer,
'Mang them as bairnies we wad often hide.

The peewits i the Spring, abuin the plooin
Swooped an dived and caa'd sae loud an shrill;
Across the hill the plaintiff whaups were cryin;
Sae sweet the laverock's sang at gloamin still.

When the cauld north wind blew i the Winter,
And aa the stars were glitterin sherp an clear,
The northern sky seemed fou o rare enchantment,
As the Merry Dancers flitted far an near.

An so I'll save for the day I'm shair is comin,
When I, wi happy hert, haud aff for hame;
Tae see again the faces aa familiar;
Ca the auld places by their weel-kent name!

whaups – *curlews*
laverock – *skylark*
haud aff – *set off*

H.S. Kinnaird
Rhymes Frae the Ochils